HEROIC JOBS

SPECIAL FORCES

Ellen Labrecque

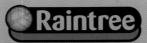
Raintree

Chicago, Illinois

www.capstonepub.com
Visit our website to find out more information about Heinemann-Raintree books.

To order:
☎ Phone 888-454-2279
💻 Visit www.capstonepub.com
   to browse our catalog and order online.

Edited by Dan Nunn, Rebecca Rissman, and Catherine Veitch
Designed by Joanne Malivoire
Picture research by Elizabeth Alexander
Originated by Capstone Global Library
Printed and bound in China by CTPS

15 14 13 12
10 9 8 7 6 5 4 3 2

Library of Congress Cataloging-in-Publication Data
Labrecque, Ellen.
  Special forces / Ellen Labrecque.
    p. cm.—(Heroic jobs)
  Includes bibliographical references and index.
  ISBN 978-1-4109-4359-0 (hb)—ISBN 978-1-4109-4366-8 (pb) 1. Special forces (Military science)—United States—Juvenile literature. 2. Special operations (Military science)—Juvenile literature. I. Title.
  UA34.S64L33 2012
  356'.160973—dc22   2011015759

Acknowledgments
We would like to thank the following for permission to reproduce photographs: Alamy pp. 11 (© MARKA), 15 (© vario images GmbH & Co.KG), 27 (© Jochen Tack), 29 (© Captured Sight); Corbis pp. 4 (© Chad Hunt), 16 (Andrea Comas/Reuters), 21 (© Christopher Morris/VII), 22 (Demotix), 24 (© THAIER AL-SUDANI/Reuters), 28 (Demotix); Getty Images pp. 8 (Jack Guez/AFP), 9 (WISSAM AL-OKAILI/AFP), 10 (John Moore), 13 (Justin D. Pyle/U.S. Army), 18 (Tyler Stableford), 19 (James M. Bowman/USAF), 26 (Eric Cabanis/AFP); Photolibrary pp. 5 (StockTrek Corporation), 6 (Juergen Hasenkopf), 7 (Norbert Probst), 12 (StockTrek Corporation), 20 (Das Fotoarchiv); Photoshot p.14 (WpN/UPPA); Shutterstock pp.17 (© Pedro Jorge Henriques Monteiro), 23 (© Ragne Kabanova), 25 (© Ivan Cholakov Gostock-dot-net).

Cover photograph of a helicopter evac required for British troops in Afghanistan, reproduced with permission of Alamy (© Stephen Mulcahey).

The faces of some of the soldiers in this book have been covered or blurred to protect their identities.

Some words are shown in bold, **like this**. You can find out what they mean by looking in the glossary.

Contents

Rescue Mission

A helicopter flies through the air. A pilot, copilot, and two special force **operatives** are inside. The helicopter door slides open and the operatives slide down a cable and land safely on the ground. The special force operation begins!

What Are Special Forces?

The special forces are soldiers who do the most dangerous jobs in the world. They do jobs such as fighting and spying, rescue missions, and disposing of bombs before they explode. Sometimes they work alone. But more often, they work in a team with other brave soldiers.

These soldiers are training for an underwater attack. They use special equipment to breathe underwater.

Meet the Special Force Operatives

Special force soldiers really care about their jobs. They are very smart and fit. They also feel comfortable talking to people from different cultures.

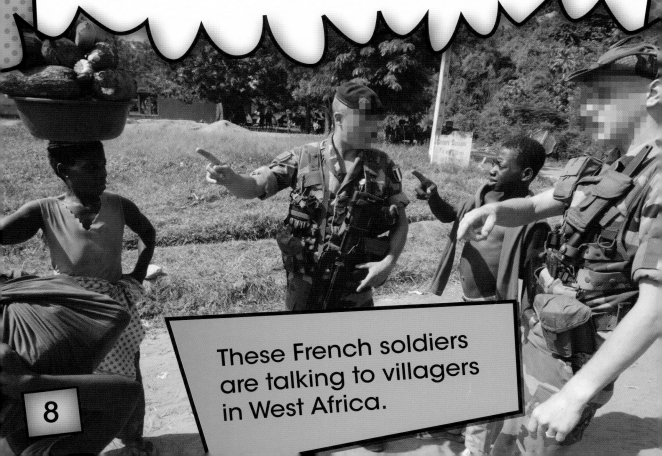

These French soldiers are talking to villagers in West Africa.

Did you know?

Most special force **operatives** speak many languages. This helps them talk to and fit in with local people.

9

Task Force Teams

Special force **operatives** are assigned to **task forces**. A task force is a group of people working for one leader to carry out a mission. Some task forces work to capture **terrorists**. Terrorists are people who use violence to get what they want.

Task forces work together with one goal in mind.

Special force **operatives** put their lives in danger. One of the biggest dangers comes from going into enemy **territory**. If an enemy discovers and captures a soldier, he or she could be killed.

Soldiers work in secret and often at night.

Equipment

Special force operations use cool equipment that you might have seen in movies. A plasma knife helps stop bleeding when put into a wound. It heats and melts the skin to create a bandage!

Night vision
goggles

Did you know?
Night vision goggles and
binoculars help soldiers to see
at night, without being seen.

15

Reconnaissance

The most important job in any military operation is called **reconnaissance**. This means watching the enemy to find out information about them. Special forces and other soldiers also gather facts about the weather and landscape of the country. The more they know, the more successful the operation will be.

Spying

Sometimes **operatives** secretly find out information about their enemy by pretending to be somebody else. This is called spying. The spies dress, act, and speak as much like the local people as possible. The information might help them during an investigation or in battle.

Preventing Terrorism

Special force **operatives** work to stop **terrorists** before they can carry out an attack. Many lives have been saved because of these operations. The **task forces** often use information from local people to do their job well. It is important for people to trust them.

These soldiers are knocking down a door as a **suspected** terrorist is inside.

Tracking Down Terrorists

Sometimes, **terrorists** do manage to carry out their attacks. Then they must be caught to stop them from attacking again. Terrorists hide all over the world. They hide in mountain areas and in cities. Tracking them down is a dangerous and difficult job.

Did you know?
Special forces can find terrorists by tracking their cell phones.

23

Defusing Bombs

Most people would run away from a bomb. Special operation bomb squads run towards a bomb. Their job is to **defuse**, or stop, the bomb from exploding. **Operatives** who defuse bombs need special training to learn their skills.

One wrong move and the operative's own life and the lives of others could be lost.

Sometimes operatives explode bombs in carefully controlled explosions.

25

Rescuing Hostages

A **hostage** is a person captured by an enemy and held until demands are met. Hostage rescue teams are trained to rescue hostages without giving in to the enemy's demands. They will sometimes make a deal, or **negotiate**, with captors. But usually, the teams try to rescue hostages.

Best of the Best

Special forces are called "special" because they are! All soldiers must be brave, but special force **operatives** are the most highly trained soldiers of all. They are highly skilled and perform the most dangerous tasks in the world. Soldiers can't just sign up to become special operatives. They are chosen because of their special talents.

Glossary

defuse stop a bomb from exploding by removing the fuse

hostage person captured by an enemy and held until demands are met

negotiate deal or bargain with

operative person skilled in a certain type of work

reconnaissance watching the enemy to find out information about them

suspected person thought to have done wrong

task force group of people working under one leader to carry out a mission

territory land that is owned or controlled

terrorist person who uses violence to get what he or she wants

Find Out More

Books

Covert, Kim. *U.S. Air Force Special Forces: Para Rescue*. Mankato, Minn.: Capstone Press, 2000.

Ferguson, Amanda. *Inside Special Operations: British Special Air Service*. New York: Rosen Publishing Group, 2003.

Websites

www.goarmy.com/special-forces.html
This is part of the U.S. Army website that is dedicated to the special forces.

army.mod.uk/
This is the British Army website.

Index